SHAMBHALA
CLASSICS

Books by J. Krishnamurti

Can Humanity Change?: J. Krishnamurti in Dialogue with Buddhists

Facing a World in Crisis: What Life Teaches Us in Challenging Times

Freedom, Love, and Action

Inward Revolution: Bringing about Radical Change in the World

Meditations

Talks with American Students

This Light in Oneself: True Meditation

To Be Human

MEDITATIONS

J. Krishnamurti

SELECTIONS MADE BY
Evelyne Blau

SHAMBHALA
Boston & London
2002

SHAMBHALA PUBLICATIONS, INC.
HORTICULTURAL HALL
300 MASSACHUSETTS AVENUE
BOSTON, MASSACHUSETTS 02115
www.shambhala.com

9 8 7 6 5 4 3

Printed in the United States of America

♾ This edition is printed on acid-free paper that meets the
American National Standards Institute z39.48 Standard.
Distributed in the United States by Random House, Inc.,
and in Canada by Random House of Canada Ltd

For more information contact:

Krishnamurti Foundation of America
Post Office Box 1560
Ojai, California 93024
U.S.A.
www.kfa.org

or

Krishnamurti Foundation Trust
Brockwood Park
Bramdean, Hampshire SO24 0LQ
England
www.kfoundation.org

LIBRARY OF CONGRESS CATALOGING-IN-PUBLICATION DATA
Krishnamurti, J. (Jiddu), 1895–
Meditations / J. Krishnamurti.—1st ed.
p. cm. —(Shambhala classics)
ISBN 978-1-57062-941-9 (pbk.: alk. paper)
L. Meditations. I. Title. II. Series
BP565.K7 M39 2002
181'.4—dc21
2002070630

FOREWORD

WHEN THE BOOK *Meditations* first appeared in 1979 the question was raised as to whether it was appropriate to excerpt passages from Krishnamurti's voluminous writings and focus on only one subject and excerpts at that. Surely, excerpts would diminish the integrity and seriousness of his teachings, it was said. After all, during his lifetime (1895–1986) Krishnamurti never spoke topically, focusing only on one theme, but rather wove many threads of contemplation into an enormous tapestry. Should one withdraw just one thread for observation and should they be excerpts, particles of the thread?

Over many years of immersion in the teachings of Krishnamurti the overarching significance of meditation becomes increasingly clear. No matter what subject is delved into, it appears that the approach is with a mind that is free of the known, of the assumptions of the past. It is only such a mind, Krishnamurti said, a meditative mind, that can inquire into such questions as fear, conflict, relationship, love, death, and, of course, meditation itself.

The writings in this newly expanded edition consist of additional material gleaned from talks, writings, and diary notes, some of which have never before been published. They represent an astonishing outpouring which illustrates the deep meaning meditation had in the life of J. Krishnamurti.

PREFACE

MAN, IN ORDER TO ESCAPE his conflicts, has invented many forms of meditation. These have been based on desire, will and the urge for achievement, and imply conflict and a struggle to arrive. This conscious, deliberate striving is always within the limits of a conditioned mind and in this there is no freedom. All effort to meditate is the denial of meditation.

Meditation is the ending of thought. It is only then that there is a different dimension which is beyond time.

J. KRISHNAMURTI
March 1979

MEDITATIONS

A MEDITATIVE MIND IS SILENT. It is not the silence which thought can conceive of; it is not the silence of a still evening; it is the silence when thought—with all its images, its words and perceptions—has entirely ceased. This meditative mind is the religious mind—the religion that is not touched by the church, the temples or by chants.

The religious mind is the explosion of love. It is this love that knows no separation. To it, far is near. It is not the one or the many, but rather that state of love in which all division ceases. Like beauty, it is not of the measure of words. From this silence alone the meditative mind acts.

MEDITATION IS ONE of the greatest arts in life—perhaps the greatest, and one cannot possibly learn it from anybody. That is the beauty of it. It has no technique and therefore no authority. When you learn about yourself, watch yourself, watch the way you walk, how you eat, what you say, the gossip, the hate, the jealousy—if you are aware of all that in yourself, without any choice, that is part of meditation.

So meditation can take place when you are sitting in a bus or walking in the woods full of light and shadows, or listening to the singing of birds or looking at the face of your wife or child.

IT'S CURIOUS how all-important meditation becomes; there's no end to it nor is there a beginning to it. It's like a raindrop: in that drop are all the streams, the great rivers, the seas and the waterfalls; that drop nourishes the earth and man; without it, the earth would be a desert. Without meditation the heart becomes a desert, a wasteland.

MEDITATION IS to find out whether the brain, with all the activities, all its experiences, can be absolutely quiet. Not forced, because the moment you force, there is duality. The entity that says, "I would like to have marvelous experiences, therefore I must force my brain to be quiet," will never do it. But if you begin to inquire, observe, listen to all the movements of thought, its conditioning, its pursuits, its fears, its pleasures, watch how the brain operates, then you will see that the brain becomes extraordinarily quiet; that quietness is not sleep but is tremendously active and therefore quiet. A big dynamo that is working perfectly hardly makes a sound; it is only when there is friction that there is noise.

SILENCE AND SPACIOUSNESS go together. The immensity of silence is the immensity of the mind in which a center does not exist.

MEDITATION IS HARD WORK. It demands the highest form of discipline—not conformity, not imitation, not obedience—but a discipline which comes through constant awareness, not only of the things about you outwardly, but also inwardly. So meditation is not an activity of isolation but is action in everyday life which demands co-operation, sensitivity and intelligence. Without laying the foundation of a righteous life, meditation becomes an escape and therefore has no value whatsoever. A righteous life is not the following of social morality, but the freedom from envy, greed and the search for power—which all breed enmity. The freedom from these does not come through the activity of will but by being aware of them through self-knowing. Without knowing the activities of the self, meditation becomes sensuous excitement and therefore of very little significance.

ALWAYS TO SEEK for wider, deeper, transcendental experiences is a form of escape from the actual reality of "what is," which is ourselves, our own conditioned mind. A mind that is awake, intelligent, free, why should it need, why should it have, any experience at all? Light is light; it does not ask for more light.

MEDITATION IS ONE of the most extraordinary things, and if you do not know what it is you are like the blind man in a world of bright color, shadows and moving light. It is not an intellectual affair, but when the heart enters into the mind, the mind has quite a different quality; it is really, then, limitless, not only in its capacity to think, to act efficiently, but also in its sense of living in a vast space where you are part of everything.

Meditation is the movement of love. It isn't the love of the one or of the many. It is like water that anyone can drink out of any jar, whether golden or earthenware; it is inexhaustible. And a peculiar thing takes place, which no drug or self-hypnosis can bring about; it is as though the mind enters into itself, beginning at the surface and penetrating ever more deeply, until depth and height have lost their meaning and every form of measurement ceases. In this state there is complete peace—not contentment which has come about through gratification—but a peace that has order, beauty and intensity. It can all be destroyed, as you can destroy a flower, and yet because of its very vulnerability it is indestructible. This meditation cannot be learned from another. You must begin without knowing anything about it, and move from innocence to innocence.

The soil in which the meditative mind can begin is the soil of everyday life, the strife, the pain and the fleeting joy. It must begin there, and bring order, and from there move endlessly. But if you are concerned only with making order, then that very order will bring about its own limitation, and the mind will be its prisoner. In all this movement you must somehow

begin from the other end, from the other shore, and not always be concerned with this shore or how to cross the river.
You must take a plunge into the water, not knowing how to
swim. And the beauty of meditation is that you never know
where you are, where you are going, what the end is.

MEDITATION IS not something different from daily life; do not go off into the corner of a room and meditate for ten minutes, then come out of it and be a butcher—both metaphorically and actually.

IF YOU SET OUT TO MEDITATE, it will not be meditation. If you set out to be good, goodness will never flower. If you cultivate humility, it ceases to be. Meditation is the breeze that comes in when you leave the window open; but if you deliberately keep it open, deliberately invite it to come, it will never appear.

MEDITATION is not a means to an end. It is both the means and the end.

WHAT AN EXTRAORDINARY thing meditation is. If there
is any kind of compulsion, effort to make thought conform,
imitate, then it becomes a wearisome burden. The silence
which is desired ceases to be illuminating. If it is the pursuit of
visions and experiences, then it leads to illusions and self-
hypnosis. Only in the flowering of thought and so ending
thought does meditation have significance. Thought can only
flower in freedom, not in ever-widening patterns of knowledge. Knowledge may give newer experiences of greater sen-
sation but a mind that is seeking experiences of any kind is
immature. Maturity is the freedom from all experience; it is
no longer under any influence to be or not to be.

Maturity in meditation is the freeing of the mind from
knowledge, for knowledge shapes and controls all experience.
A mind which is a light to itself needs no experience. Immaturity is the craving for greater and wider experience. Meditation is the wandering through the world of knowledge and
being free of it to enter into the unknown.

ONE HAS TO FIND OUT for oneself, not through anybody. We have had the authority of teachers, saviors and masters. If you really want to find out what meditation is, you have to set aside all authority completely.

HAPPINESS AND PLEASURE you can buy in any market at a price, but bliss you cannot buy—either for yourself or for another. Happiness and pleasure are time-binding. Only in total freedom does bliss exist. Pleasure, like happiness, you can seek and find in many ways, but they come and go. Bliss—that strange sense of joy—has no motive. You cannot possibly seek it. Once it is there, depending on the quality of your mind, it remains—timeless, causeless, a thing that is not measurable by time. Meditation is not the pursuit of pleasure or the search for happiness. Meditation, on the contrary, is a state of mind in which there is no concept or formula, and therefore total freedom. It is only to such a mind that this bliss comes—unsought and uninvited. Once it is there, though you may live in the world with all its noise, pleasure and brutality, they will not touch that mind. Once it is there, conflict has ceased. But the ending of conflict is not necessarily total freedom. Meditation is the movement of the mind in this freedom. In this explosion of bliss the eyes are made innocent, and love is then benediction.

I DO NOT KNOW if you have ever noticed that when you give total attention there is complete silence. And in that attention there is no frontier, there is no center, as the "me" who is aware or attentive. That attention, that silence, is a state of meditation.

WE HARDLY EVER LISTEN to the sound of a dog's bark or to the cry of a child or the laughter of a man as he passes by. We separate ourselves from everything, and then from this isolation look and listen to all things. It is this separation that is so destructive, for in that lies all conflict and confusion. If you listened to the sound of bells with complete silence you would be riding on it—or, rather, the sound would carry you across the valley and over the hill. The beauty of it is felt only when you and the sound are not separate, when you are part of it. Meditation is the ending of the separation, but not by any action of will or desire.

Meditation is not a separate thing from life; it is the very essence of life, the very essence of daily living. To listen to the bells, to hear the laughter of a peasant as he walks by with his wife, to listen to the sound of the bell on the bicycle of a little girl as she passes by: it is the whole of life, and not just a fragment of it, that meditation opens.

joy

MEDITATION is the seeing of "what is" and going beyond it.

PERCEPTION WITHOUT the word, that is without thought, is one of the strangest phenomena. Then the perception is much more acute, not only with the brain, but with all the senses. Such perception is not the fragmentary perception of the intellect nor the affair of the emotions. It can be called a total perception, and it is part of meditation. Perception without the perceiver in meditation is to commune with the height and depth of the immense. This perception is entirely different from seeing an object without an observer, because in the perception of meditation there is no object and therefore no experience. Meditation can take place when the eyes are open and one is surrounded by objects of every kind, but then these objects have no importance at all. One sees them but there is no process of recognition, which means there is no experiencing.

What meaning has such meditation? There is no meaning; there is no utility. But in that meditation there is a movement of great ecstasy, which is not to be confounded with pleasure. It is the ecstasy, which gives to the eye, to the brain, and to the heart the quality of innocence. Without seeing life as something totally new, it is a routine, boredom, and a meaningless affair. So meditation is of the greatest importance. It opens the door to the incalculable, the measureless.

MEDITATION IS NEVER in time; time cannot bring about mutation. Time can bring about change, which then needs to be changed again, like all reforms. Meditation that springs out of time is always binding; there is no freedom in it and without freedom there is always choice and conflict.

WE HAVE TO ALTER the structure of our society, its injustice, its appalling morality, the divisions it has created between man and man, the wars, the utter lack of affection and love that is destroying the world. If your meditation is only a personal matter, a thing which you personally enjoy, then it is not meditation. Meditation implies a complete radical change of the mind and the heart. This is only possible when there is this extraordinary sense of inward silence, and that alone brings about the religious mind. That mind knows what is sacred.

WE ARE INQUIRING together, as to whether you and I, on the instant, can completely change and enter into a totally different dimension—and that involves meditation. Meditation is something that demands a great deal of intelligence, a sensitivity and the capacity of love and beauty—not just the following of a system invented by some guru.

TO MEDITATE is to be innocent of time.

MEDITATION IS NOT AN ESCAPE from the world; it is not an isolating, self-enclosing activity, but rather the comprehension of the world and its ways. The world has little to offer apart from food, clothes and shelter, and pleasure with its great sorrows.

Meditation is wandering away from this world. One has to be a total outsider, then the world has a meaning, and the beauty of the heavens and the earth is constant. Then love is not pleasure. From this, all action begins that is not the outcome of tension, contradiction, the search for self-fulfillment or the conceit of power.

IF YOU DELIBERATELY take an attitude, a posture, in order to meditate, then it becomes a plaything, a toy of the mind. If you determine to extricate yourself from the confusion and the misery of life, then it becomes an experience of imagination—and this is not meditation. The conscious mind or the unconscious mind must have no part in it; they must not even be aware of the extent and beauty of meditation—if they are, then you might just as well go and buy a romantic novel.

In the total attention of meditation there is no knowing, no recognition, nor the remembrance of something that has happened. Time and thought have entirely come to an end, for they are the center, which limits its own vision.

At the moment of light, thought withers away, and the conscious effort to experience and the remembrance of it is the word that has been. And the word is never the actual. At that moment—which is not of time—the ultimate is the immediate, but that ultimate has no symbol, is of no person, of no god.

MEDITATION IS to find out if there is a field, which is not already contaminated by the known.

MEDITATION IS THE FLOWERING of understanding. Understanding is not within the borders of time; time never brings understanding. Understanding is not a gradual process to be gathered little by little, with care and patience.

Understanding is now or never; it is a destructive flash, not a tame affair; it is this shattering that one is afraid of and so one avoids it, knowingly or unknowingly. Understanding may alter the course of one's life, the way of thought and action; it may be pleasant or not, but understanding is a danger to all relationship. Without understanding, sorrow will continue. Sorrow ends only through self-knowing, the awareness of every thought and feeling, every movement of the conscious and of that which is hidden. Meditation is the understanding of consciousness, the hidden and the open, and of the movement that lies beyond all thought and feeling.

IT WAS ONE of those lovely mornings that have never been before. The sun was just coming up and you saw it between the eucalyptus and the pine. It was over the waters, golden, burnished—such light that exists only between the mountains and the sea. It was such a clear morning, breathless, full of that strange light that one sees not only with one's eyes but with one's heart. And when you see it the heavens are very close to earth, and you are lost in the beauty. You know, you should never meditate in public, or with another, or in a group; you should meditate only in solitude, in the quiet of the night or in the still, early morning. When you meditate in solitude, it must be solitude. You must be completely alone, not following a system, a method, repeating words, pursuing a thought, or shaping a thought according to your desire.

This solitude comes when the mind is freed from thought. When there are influences of desire or of the things that the mind is pursuing, either in the future or in the past, there is no solitude. Only in the immensity of the present this aloneness comes. And then in quiet secrecy in which all communication has come to an end, in which there is no observer with his anxieties, with his stupid appetites and problems—only then, in that quiet aloneness, meditation becomes something that cannot be put into words. Then meditation is an eternal movement.

I don't know if you have ever meditated, if you have ever been alone, by yourself, far away from everything, from every person, from every thought and pursuit, if you have ever been completely alone, not isolated, not withdrawn into some fanciful dream or vision, but far away, so that in yourself there is nothing recognizable, nothing that you touch by thought or feeling, so far away that in this full solitude the very silence becomes the only flower, the only light, and the timeless quality that is not measurable by thought. Only in such meditation love has its being. Don't bother to express it; it will express itself. Don't use it. Don't try to put it into action; it will act, and when it acts, in that action will be no regret, no contradiction, none of the misery and travail of man.

So meditate alone. Get lost. And don't try to remember where you have been. If you try to remember it, then it will be something that is dead. And if you hold on to the memory of it, then you will never be alone again. So meditate in that endless solitude, in the beauty of that love, in that innocence, in the new—then there is the bliss that is imperishable.

The sky is very blue, the blue that comes after the rain, and these rains have come after many months of drought. After the rain the skies are washed clean and the hills are rejoicing, and the earth is still. And every leaf has the light of the sun on it, and the feeling of the earth is very close to you. So meditate in the very secret recesses of your heart and mind, where you have never been before.

MEDITATION IS NOT A MEANS to an end; there is no end, no arrival; it is a movement in time and out of time. Every system, method, binds thought to time, but choiceless awareness of every thought and feeling, understanding of their motives, their mechanism, allowing them to blossom, is the beginning of meditation. When thought and feeling flourish and die, meditation is the movement beyond time. In this movement there is ecstasy; in complete emptiness there is love, and with love there is destruction and creation.

MEDITATION is that light in the mind which lights the way for action; and without that light there is no love.

MEDITATION IS NEVER PRAYER. Prayer, supplication, is born of self-pity. You pray when you are in difficulty, when there is sorrow; but when there is happiness, joy, there is no supplication. This self-pity, so deeply embedded in man, is the root of separation. That which is separate, or thinks itself separate, ever seeking identification with something that is not separate, brings only more division and pain. Out of this confusion one cries to heaven, or to one's husband, or to some deity of the mind. This cry may find an answer, but the answer is the echo of self-pity, in its separation.

The repetition of words, of prayers, is self-hypnotic, self-enclosing and destructive. The isolation of thought is always within the field of the known, and the answer to prayer is the response of the known.

Meditation is far from this. In this field, thought cannot enter; there is no separation, and so no identity. Meditation is in the open; secrecy has no place in it. Everything is exposed, clear; then the beauty of love is.

ON THIS MORNING the quality of meditation was nothingness, the total emptiness of time and space. It is a fact and not an idea or the paradox of opposing speculations. One finds this strange emptiness when the root of all problems withers away. This root is thought, the thought that divides and holds. In meditation the mind actually becomes empty of the past, though it can use the past as thought. This goes on throughout the day and at night sleep is the emptiness of yesterday and therefore the mind touches that which is timeless.

MEDITATION is not the mere control of body and thought, nor is it a system of breathing in and breathing out. The body must be still, healthy and without strain; sensitivity of feeling must be sharpened and sustained; and the mind with all its chattering, disturbances and gropings must come to an end. It is not the organism that one must begin with, but rather it is the mind with its opinions, prejudices and self-interest that must be seen to. When the mind is healthy, vital and vigorous, then feeling will be heightened and will be extremely sensitive. Then the body, with its own natural intelligence, which hasn't been spoiled by habit and taste, will function as it should.

So one must begin with the mind and not with the body, the mind being thought and the varieties of expressions of thought. Mere concentration makes thought narrow, limited and brittle, but concentration comes as a natural thing when there is an awareness of the ways of thought. This awareness does not come from the thinker who chooses and discards, who holds on to and rejects. This awareness is without choice and is both the outer and the inner; it is an interflow between the two, so the division between the outer and the inner comes to an end.

Thought destroys feeling—feeling being love. Thought can offer only pleasure, and in the pursuit of pleasure love is pushed aside. The pleasure of eating, of drinking, has its continuity in thought, and merely to control or suppress this pleasure which thought has brought about has no meaning; it creates only various forms of conflict and compulsion.

Thought, which is matter, cannot seek that which is beyond

time, for thought is memory, and the experience in that memory is as dead as the leaf of last autumn.

In awareness of all this comes attention, which is not the product of inattention. It is inattention, which has dictated the pleasurable habits of the body and diluted the intensity of feeling. Inattention cannot be made into attention. The awareness of inattention is attention.

The seeing of this whole complex process is meditation, from which alone comes order in this confusion. This order is as absolute as is the order in mathematics, and from this there is action—the immediate doing. Order is not arrangement, design and proportion; these come much later. Order comes out of a mind that is not cluttered up by the things of thought. When thought is silent, there is emptiness, which is order.

IT WAS REALLY a marvelous river, wide, deep, with so many cities on its banks, so carelessly free and yet never abandoning itself. All life was there upon its banks, green fields, forests, solitary houses, death, love and destruction; there were long, wide bridges over it, graceful and well-used. Other streams and rivers joined it but she was the mother of all rivers, the little ones and the big ones. She was always full, ever purifying herself, and of an evening it was a blessing to watch her, with deepening color in the clouds and her waters golden. But the little trickle so far away, amongst those gigantic rocks, which seemed so concentrated in producing it, was the beginning of life, and its ending was beyond its banks and the seas.

Meditation was like that river, only it had no beginning and no ending; it began and its ending was its beginning. There was no cause and its movement was its renewal. It was always new, it never gathered to become old; it never got sullied for it had no roots in time. It is good to meditate, not forcing it, not making any effort, beginning with a trickle and going beyond time and space, where thought and feeling cannot enter, where experience is not.

MEDITATION is the total release of energy.

IN THE SPACE which thought creates around itself there is no love. This space divides man from man, and in it is all the becoming, the battle of life, the agony and fear. Meditation is the ending of this space, the ending of the "me." Then relationship has quite a different meaning, for in that space which is not made by thought, the other does not exist, for you do not exist.

Meditation, then, is not the pursuit of some vision, however sanctified by tradition. Rather it is the endless space where thought cannot enter. To us, the little space made by thought around itself, which is the "me," is extremely important, for this is all the mind knows, identifying itself with everything that is in that space. And the fear of not being is born in that space. But in meditation, when this is understood, the mind can enter into a dimension of space where action is inaction.

We do not know what love is, for in the space made by thought around itself as the "me," love is the conflict of the "me" and the "not-me." This conflict, this torture, is not love.

Thought is the very denial of love, and it cannot enter into that space where the "me" is not. In that space is the benediction which man seeks and cannot find. He seeks it within the frontiers of thought, and thought destroys the ecstasy of this benediction.

BELIEF IS SO UNNECESSARY, as are ideals. Both dissipate energy which is needed to follow the unfolding of the fact, the "what is." Beliefs, like ideals, are escapes from the fact and in escape there is no end to sorrow. The ending of sorrow is the understanding of the fact from moment to moment. There is no system or method which will give understanding but only a choiceless awareness of a fact. Meditation according to a system is the avoidance of the fact of what you are; it is far more important to understand yourself, the constant changing of the facts about yourself, than to meditate in order to find god, have visions, sensations, and other forms of entertainment.

MEDITATION AT THAT HOUR was freedom and it was like entering into an unknown world of beauty and quietness; it was a world without image, symbol or word, without waves of memory. Love was the death of every minute and each death was the renewing of love. It was not attachment, it had no roots; it flowered without cause and it was a flame that burned away the borders, the carefully built fences of consciousness. It was beauty beyond thought and feeling; it was not put together on canvas, in words or in marble. Meditation was joy and with it came a benediction.

THE FLOWERING of love is meditation.

IN MEDITATION one has to find out whether there is an end to knowledge and so freedom from the known.

IT HAD RAINED HEAVILY during the night and the day, and down the gullies the muddy stream poured into the sea, making it chocolate-brown. As you walked on the beach the waves were enormous and they were breaking with magnificent curve and force. You walked against the wind, and suddenly you felt there was nothing between you and the sky, and this openness was heaven. To be so completely open, vulnerable— to the hills, to the sea and to man—is the very essence of meditation.

To have no resistance, to have no barriers inwardly towards anything, to be really free, completely, from all the minor urges, compulsions and demands, with all their little conflicts and hypocrisies, is to walk in life with open arms. And that evening, walking there on that wet sand, with the sea gulls around you, you felt the extraordinary sense of open freedom and the great beauty of love which was not in you or outside you—but everywhere.

We don't realize how important it is to be free of the nagging pleasures and their pains, so that the mind remains alone. It is only the mind that is wholly alone that is open. You felt all this suddenly, like a great wind that swept over the land and through you. There you were—denuded of everything, empty—and therefore utterly open. The beauty of it was not in the word or in the feeling, but seemed to be everywhere— about you, inside you, over the waters and in the hills. Meditation is this.

MEDITATION IS NOT concentration, which is exclusion, a cutting off, a resistance and so a conflict. A meditative mind can concentrate, which then is not an exclusion, a resistance, but a concentrated mind cannot meditate.

IN THE UNDERSTANDING of meditation there is love, and love is not the product of systems, of habits, of following a method. Love cannot be cultivated by thought. Love can perhaps come into being when there is complete silence, a silence in which the meditator is entirely absent; and the mind can be silent only when it understands its own movement as thought and feeling. To understand this movement of thought and feeling there can be no condemnation in observing it. To observe in such a way is a discipline, and that kind of discipline is fluid, free, not the discipline of conformity.

THAT MORNING the sea was like a lake or an enormous river—without a ripple, and so calm that you could see the reflections of the stars so early in the morning. The dawn had not yet come, so the stars, the reflection of the cliff and the distant lights of the town were there on the water. And as the sun came up over the horizon in a cloudless sky it made a golden path, and it was extraordinary to see that light of California filling the earth and every leaf and blade of grass.

As you watched, a great stillness came into you. The brain itself became very quiet, without any reaction, without a movement, and it was strange to feel this immense stillness. "Feel" isn't the word. The quality of that silence, that stillness, is not felt by the brain; it is beyond the brain. The brain can conceive, formulate or make a design for the future, but this stillness is beyond its range, beyond all imagination, beyond all desire. You are so still that your body becomes completely part of the earth, part of everything that is still.

And as the slight breeze came from the hills, stirring the leaves, this stillness, this extraordinary quality of silence, was not disturbed. The house was between the hills and the sea, overlooking the sea. And as you watched the sea, so very still, you really became part of everything. You were everything. You were the light, and the beauty of love. Again, to say "you were a part of everything" is also wrong: the word "you" is not adequate because you really weren't there. You didn't exist. There was only that stillness, the beauty, the extraordinary sense of love.

THE WORDS "you" and "I" separate things. This division in this strange silence and stillness doesn't exist. And as you watched out of the window, space and time seemed to have come to an end, and the space that divides had no reality. That leaf and that eucalyptus and the blue shining water were not different from you.

Meditation is really very simple. We complicate it. We weave a web of ideas around it—what it is and what it is not. But it is none of these things. Because it is so very simple it escapes us, because our minds are so complicated, so timeworn and time-based. And this mind dictates the activity of the heart, and then the trouble begins. But meditation comes naturally, with extraordinary ease, when you walk on the sand or look out of your window or see those marvelous hills burnt by last summer's sun. Why are we such tortured human beings, with tears in our eyes and false laughter on our lips? If you could walk alone among those hills or in the woods or along the long, white, bleached sands, in that solitude you would know what meditation is.

The ecstasy of solitude comes when you are not frightened to be alone—no longer belonging to the world or attached to anything. Then, like that dawn that came up this morning, it comes silently, and makes a golden path in the very stillness, which was at the beginning, which is now, and which will be always there.

MEDITATION IS a movement in and of the unknown. You are not there, only the movement. You are too petty or too great for this movement. It has nothing behind it or in front of it. It is that energy which thought-matter cannot touch. Thought is perversion, for it is the product of yesterday; it is caught in the toils of centuries and so is confused, unclear. Do what you will, the known cannot reach out for the unknown. Meditation is the dying to the known.

THE MEDITATION of a mind that is utterly silent is the benediction that man is ever seeking. In this silence every quality of
silence is.

ONCE YOU HAVE LAID the foundation of virtue, which is order in relationship, there comes into being this quality of love and of dying, which is all of life; then the mind becomes extraordinarily quiet, naturally silent, not made silent through suppression, discipline and control, and that silence is immensely rich.

Beyond that, no word, no description is of any avail. Then the mind does not inquire into the absolute because it has no need, for in that silence there is that which is. And the whole of this is the benediction of meditation.

AFTER THE RAINS the hills were splendid. They were still brown from the summer sun, and soon all the green things would come out. It had rained quite heavily, and the beauty of those hills was indescribable. The sky was still clouded and in the air there was the smell of sumac, sage and eucalyptus. It was splendid to be among them, and a strange stillness possessed you. Unlike the sea, which lay far down below you, those hills were completely still. As you watched and looked about you, you had left everything down below in that little house—your clothes, your thoughts and the odd ways of life. Here you were travelling very lightly, without any thoughts, without any burden, and with a feeling of complete emptiness and beauty. The little green bushes would soon be still greener, and in a few weeks' time they would have a stronger smell. The quails were calling and a few of them flew over. Without knowing it, the mind was in a state of meditation in which love was flowering. After all, only in the soil of meditation can this flower bloom. It was really quite marvelous and, strangely, all through the night it pursued you, and when you woke, long before the sun was up, it was still there in your heart with its incredible joy, for no reason whatsoever. It was there, causeless, and quite intoxicating. It would be there all through the day without your ever asking or inviting it to stay with you.

THERE ON THE PERFUMED VERANDAH, when dawn was still far away and the trees were still silent, what is essence is beauty. But this essence is not experienceable; experiencing must cease, for experience only strengthens the known. The known is never the essence. Meditation is never the further experiencing; it is not only the ending of experience, which is the response to challenge, great or small, but it is the opening of the door to essence, opening the door of a furnace whose fire utterly destroys, without leaving any ashes; there are no remains. We are the remains, the yes-sayers of many thousand yesterdays, a continuous series of endless memories, of choice and despair. The Big Self and the Little Self are the pattern of existence and existence is thought and thought is existence, with never-ending sorrow. In the flame of meditation thought ends and with it feeling, for neither is love. Without love, there is no essence; without it there are only ashes on which is based our existence. Out of the emptiness love is.

MEDITATION is the action of silence.

MEDITATION HAS no beginning and no end; in it there is no achievement and no failure, no gathering and no renunciation; it is a movement without finality and so beyond and above time and space. The experiencing of it is the denying of it, for the experiencer is bound to time and space, memory and recognition. The foundation for true meditation is that passive awareness which is the total freedom from authority and ambition, envy and fear. Meditation has no meaning, no significance whatsoever without this freedom, without self-knowing; as long as there is choice there is no self-knowing. Choice implies conflict, which prevents the understanding of "what is." Wandering off into some fancy, into some romantic beliefs, is not meditation; the brain must strip itself of every myth, illusion and security and face the reality of their falseness. There is no distraction; everything is in the movement of meditation. The flower is the form, the scent, the color, and the beauty that is the whole of it. Tear it to pieces actually or verbally, then there is no flower, only a remembrance of what was, which is never the flower. Meditation is the whole flower in its beauty, withering and living.

MEDITATION is the freedom from thought, and a movement in the ecstasy of truth.

IT WAS VERY QUIET so early in the morning and not a bird or leaf was stirring. Meditation which began at unknown depths, and went on with increasing intensity and sweep, carved the brain into total silence, scooping out the depths of thought, uprooting feeling, emptying the brain of the known and its shadow. It was an operation and there was no operator, no surgeon; it was going on, as a surgeon operates for cancer, cutting out every tissue which has been contaminated, lest the contamination should again spread. It was going on, this meditation, for an hour by the watch. And it was meditation without the meditator. The meditator interferes with his stupidities and vanities, ambitions and greed. The meditator is thought, nurtured in these conflicts and injuries, and thought in meditation must totally cease. This is the foundation of meditation.

TO MEDITATE is to transcend time. Time is the distance that thought travels in its achievements. The travelling is always along the old path covered over with a new coating, new sights, but always the same road, leading nowhere—except to pain and sorrow.

It is only when the mind transcends time that truth ceases to be an abstraction. Then bliss is not an idea derived from pleasure but an actuality that is not verbal.

The emptying of the mind of time is the silence of truth, and the seeing of this is the doing; so there is no division between the seeing and the doing. In the interval between seeing and doing is born conflict, misery and confusion. That which has no time is the everlasting.

DAWN WAS SLOW in coming; the stars were still brilliant and the trees were still withdrawn; no bird was calling, not even the small owls that rattled through the night from tree to tree. It was strangely quiet except for the roar of the sea. There was that smell of many flowers, rotting leaves and damp ground; the air was very, very still and the smell was everywhere. The earth was waiting for the dawn and the coming day; there was expectation, patience and a strange stillness. Meditation went on with that stillness and that stillness was love; it was not the love of something or of someone, the image and the symbol, the word and the pictures. It was simply love, without sentiment, without feeling. It was something complete in itself, naked, intense, without root and direction. The sound of that faraway bird was that love; it was the direction and distance; it was there without time and word. It wasn't an emotion that fades and is cruel; the symbol, the word can be substituted but not the thing. Being naked, it was utterly vulnerable and so indestructible. It had the unapproachable strength of that otherness, the unknowable, which was coming through the trees and beyond the sea. Meditation was the sound of that bird calling out of the emptiness and the roar of the sea, thundering against the beach. Love can only be in utter emptiness. The graying dawn was there far away on the horizon and the dark trees were even more dark and intense. In meditation there is no repetition, a continuity of habit; there is death of everything known and the flowering of the unknown. The stars had faded and the clouds were awake with the coming sun.

MEDITATION is a state of mind which looks at everything with complete attention, totally, not just parts of it.

MEDITATION IS DESTRUCTION to security, and there is great beauty in meditation, not the beauty of the things that have been put together by man or by nature but of silence. This silence is emptiness in which and from which all things flow and have their being. It is unknowable; intellect and feeling cannot make their way to it; there is no way to it and a method to it is the invention of a greedy brain. All the ways and means of the calculating self must be destroyed wholly; all going forward or backward the way of time must come to an end, without tomorrow. Meditation is destruction; it's a danger to those who wish to lead a superficial life and a life of fancy and myth.

THE DEATH that meditation brings about is the immortality of the new.

THIS IS SOMETHING most marvelous if you come upon it. I can go into it, but the description is not the described. It's for you to learn all this by looking at yourself—no book, no teacher can teach you about this. Don't depend on anyone, don't join spiritual organizations; one has to learn all this out of oneself. And there the mind will discover things that are incredible. But for that, there must be no fragmentation and therefore immense stability, swiftness, mobility. To such a mind there is no time and therefore living has quite a different meaning.

ANY AUTHORITY on meditation is the very denial of it. All the knowledge, the concepts, the examples have no place in meditation. The complete elimination of the meditator, the experiencer, the thinker, is the very essence of meditation. This freedom is the daily act of meditation. The observer is the past, his ground is time, his thoughts, images, shadows, are time-binding. Knowledge is time, and freedom from the known is the flowering of meditation. To follow another, his example, his word, is to banish truth.

Only in the mirror of relationship do you see the face of "what is." The seer is the seen. Without the order which virtue brings, meditation and the endless assertions of others have no meaning whatsoever; they are totally irrelevant. Truth has no tradition, it cannot be handed down.

DO NOT MAKE MEDITATION a complicated affair; it is really very simple and because it is simple it is very subtle. Its subtlety will escape the mind if the mind approaches it with all kinds of fanciful and romantic ideas. Meditation, really, is a penetration into the unknown, and so the known, the memory, the experience, the knowledge which it has acquired during the day, or during a thousand days, must end. For it is only a free mind that can penetrate into the very heart of the immeasurable. So meditation is both the penetration and the ending of the yesterday.

The trouble begins when we ask how to end the yesterday. There is really no "how." The "how" implies a method, a system and it is this very method and system that has conditioned the mind. Just see the truth of this. Freedom is necessary—not "how" to be free. The "how to be free" only enslaves you.

IF YOU DO NOT KNOW the meaning and the beauty of meditation you do not know anything of life. You may have the latest car, you may be able to travel all over the world freely, but if you do not know what the real beauty, the freedom and the joy of meditation is, you are missing a great part of life. Which is not to make you say, "I must learn to meditate." It is a natural thing that comes about. A mind that is inquiring must inevitably come to this; a mind that is aware, that observes "what is" in itself, is self-understanding, self-knowing.

YOU CAN SIT in the right posture with your back straight, breathing correctly, do pranayama and all the rest of it for the next ten thousand years, and you will be nowhere near perceiving what truth is, because you have not understood yourself at all, the way you think, the way you live. You have not ended your sorrow, and you want to find enlightenment. You can do all kinds of twists and turns with your body and this seems to fascinate people, because they feel it is going to give some power, some prestige. Now, all these powers are like candles in the sun; they are like candle light when the brilliant sun is shining.

TO UNDERSTAND what meditation is, one must lay the foundation of righteous behavior. Without that foundation, meditation is really a form of self-hypnosis; without being free from anger, jealousy, envy, greed, acquisitiveness, hate, competition, the desire for success—all the moral, respectable forms of what is considered righteous—without laying the right foundation, without actually living a daily life free of the distortion of personal fear, anxiety, greed and so on, meditation has very little meaning.

MEDITATION IMPLIES a quality of mind that can completely attend, therefore, a mind that can be completely still. The mind is always chattering, always talking, either to itself, within itself or to somebody, always in movement. How can a mind which is everlastingly chattering perceive anything? Only a mind that is completely attentive has the total energy to observe, because you need tremendous energy to observe. The religious monks and others say that you cannot waste energy; therefore no sex, if you want to be a saint. And when you become a celibate and have taken vows of celibacy, there is havoc in you, because you are denying the whole biological system and there is a wastage of energy. You are battling, battling, battling. Or you go to the other extreme, indulge, which is another form of wasting energy. Whereas, if you are attentive, it is the greatest form of all summation of energy. It means intensity, passion, and you cannot be passionate if you are wasting. Without any effort the mind can become completely quiet and therefore full of energy without any distortion.

MEDITATION IS a marvelous thing, if you know the meaning of a mind that is "in meditation," and not "how to meditate." We will see what meditation is not, then we will know what meditation is. Through negation you come upon the positive, but if you pursue the positive, it leads you to a dead end. We say meditation is not the practice of any system. Machines can do that. So systems cannot reveal the beauty and the depth and the marvelous thing called meditation.

MEDITATION IS NOT the repetition of the word, nor the experiencing of a vision, nor the cultivating of silence. The bead and the word do quiet the chattering mind, but this is a form of self-hypnosis. You might as well take a pill.

Meditation is not wrapping yourself in a pattern of thought, in the enchantment of pleasure. Meditation has no beginning, and therefore it has no end.

If you say, "I will begin today to control my thoughts, to sit quietly in the meditative posture, to breathe regularly," then you are caught in the tricks with which one deceives oneself. Meditation is not a matter of being absorbed in some grandiose idea or image; that only quiets one for the moment, as a child absorbed by a toy is for the time being quiet, and as soon as the toy ceases to be of interest, the restlessness and the mischief begin again. Meditation is not the pursuit of an invisible path leading to some imagined bliss. The meditative mind is seeing, watching, listening, without a word, without comment, without opinion, attentive to the movement of life in all its relationships throughout the day. And at night, when the whole organism is at rest, the meditative mind has no dreams for it has been awake all day. It is only the indolent who have dreams, only the half-asleep who need the intimation of their own states. But as the mind watches, listens to the movement of life, the outer and the inner, to such a mind comes a silence that is not put together by thought.

It is not a silence which the observer can experience. If he does experience it and recognize it, it is no longer silence. The silence of the meditative mind is not within the borders of

recognition, for this silence has no frontier. There is only silence—in which the space of division ceases.

IF I MEDITATE and continue with what I have already learned, with what I already know, then I am living in the past, within the field of my conditioning. In that there is no freedom. I may decorate the prison in which I live, I may do all kinds of things in that prison, but there is still a limitation, a barrier. So the mind has to find out whether the brain cells, which have developed through millennia, can be totally quiet, and respond to a dimension they do not know. Which means, can the mind be totally still?

PART OF MEDITATION is to eliminate totally all conflict, inwardly and therefore outwardly.

MEDITATION IMPLIES a mind that is so astonishingly clear that every form of self-deception comes to an end. One can deceive oneself infinitely; and generally meditation, so-called, is a form of self-hypnosis—the seeing of visions according to your conditioning. It is so simple: If you are a Christian you will see your Christ; if you are a Hindu you will see your Krishna, or whichever of the innumerable gods you have. But meditation is none of these things. It is the absolute stillness of the mind, the absolute quietness of the brain.

The foundation for meditation has to be laid in daily life, in how one behaves, in what one thinks. One cannot be violent and meditate; that has no meaning. If there is, psychologically, any kind of fear, then obviously meditation is an escape. For the stillness of the mind, its complete quiet, an extraordinary discipline is required; not the discipline of suppression, con-formity, or the following of some authority, but that discipline or learning which takes place throughout the day, about every movement of thought. The mind then has a religious quality of unity. From that there can be action which is not contra-dictory.

THE CURIOUS PART of meditation is that an event is not made into an experience. It is there, like a new star in the heavens, without memory taking it over and holding it, without the habitual process of recognition and response in terms of like and dislike. Our search is always outgoing; the mind seeking any experience is outgoing. Inward going is not a search at all; it is perceiving. Response is always repetitive, for it comes always from the same bank of memory.

WHAT IS IMPORTANT is not controlling thought, but understanding it, understanding the origin, the beginning of thought, which is in yourself. That is, the brain stores up memories—you can observe this yourself, you don't have to read books about it. If it had not stored up memories it would not be able to think at all. That memory is the result of experience, of knowledge—yours, or of the community, of the family, of the race and so on. Thought springs from that storehouse of memory. So thought is never free, it is always old, there is no such thing as freedom of thought. Thought can never be free in itself; it can talk about freedom, but in itself it is the result of past memories, experiences and knowledge; therefore it is old. Yet one must have this accumulation of knowledge, otherwise one could not function, one could not speak to another, could not go home, and so on. Knowledge is essential. . . .

If meditation is a continuation of knowledge, is the continuation of everything that man has accumulated, then there is no freedom. There is freedom only when there is an understanding of the function of knowledge and therefore freedom from the known.

Meditation is the emptying of consciousness of its content, the known, the "me."

IN MEDITATION, one must lay the foundation of order, which is righteousness—not respectability, the social morality which is no morality at all, but the order that comes of understanding disorder, which is quite a different thing. Disorder must exist as long as there is conflict, both outwardly and inwardly.

THERE ARE VARIOUS SCHOOLS, in India and further East, where they teach methods of meditation—it is really most appalling. It means training the mind mechanically; it therefore ceases to be free and does not understand the problem.

So when we use the word "meditation" we do not mean something that is practiced. We have no method. Meditation means awareness: to be aware of what you are doing, what you are thinking, what you are feeling, aware without any choice, to observe, to learn. Meditation is to be aware of one's conditioning, how one is conditioned by the society in which one lives, in which one has been brought up, by the religious propaganda—aware without any choice, without distortion, without wishing it were different. Out of this awareness comes attention, the capacity to be completely attentive. Then there is freedom to see things as they actually are, without distortion. The mind becomes unconfused, clear, sensitive. Such meditation brings about a quality of mind that is completely silent—of which quality one can go on talking, but it will have no meaning unless it exists.

THERE IS THE REPETITION of words, of sentences, mantras, a set of phrases given by a guru; being initiated, paying money to learn a peculiar phrase to be repeated by you secretly. Probably some of you have done that and you know a great deal about it. That is called mantra yoga, and is brought over from India. I don't know why you pay a single penny to repeat certain words from somebody who says, "If you do this you will achieve enlightenment, you will have a quiet mind." When you repeat a series of words constantly, whether it is "Ave Maria" or various Sanskrit words, obviously your mind becomes rather dull and you have a peculiar sense of unity, of quietness, and you think that will help to bring about clarity. You can see the absurdity of it, because why should you accept what anybody says about these matters—including myself? Why should you accept any authority about the inward movement of life? We reject authority outwardly; if you are at all intellectually aware and observant politically, you reject these things. But apparently we accept the authority of somebody who says, "I know, I have achieved, I have realized." The man who says he knows does not know.

VIRTUE COMES INTO BEING like a flower of goodness when you understand. Then you can begin to inquire into what it is that man has sought through the centuries, has been asking for, trying to discover. You cannot possibly understand it or come upon it if you have not laid the foundation in your daily life. And then we can ask what meditation is, not how to meditate or what steps to take to meditate, or what systems and methods to follow to meditate. All systems, all methods make the mind mechanical. If I follow a particular system, however carefully worked out by the greatest guru you can possibly imagine, that system, that method makes the mind mechanical, and a mechanical mind is a dead mind.

A SYSTEM OF MEDITATION is not meditation. A system implies a method, which you practice in order to achieve something at the end. Something practiced over and over again becomes mechanical—does it not? How can a mechanical mind, which has been trained and twisted, tortured to comply to the pattern of what it calls "meditation," hoping to achieve a reward at the end, be free to observe, to learn?

MEDITATION IS to be aware of every thought and of every feeling, never to say it is right or wrong but just to watch it and move with it. In that watching you begin to understand the whole movement of thought and feeling. And out of this awareness comes silence. Silence put together by thought is stagnation, is dead, but the silence that comes when thought has understood its own beginning, the nature of itself, understood how all thought is never free but always old—this silence is meditation in which the meditator is entirely absent, for the mind has emptied itself of the past.

MEDITATION IS never the control of the body. There is no actual division between the organism and the mind. The brain, the nervous system and the thing we call the mind are all one, indivisible. It is the natural act of meditation that brings about the harmonious movement of the whole. To divide the body from the mind and to control the body with intellectual decisions is to bring about contradiction, from which arise various forms of struggle, conflict and resistance.

WHAT IS RELIGION? It is the investigation, with all one's attention, with the summation of all one's energy, to find that which is sacred, to come upon that which is holy. That can only take place when there is freedom from the noise of thought, the ending of thought and time, psychologically, inwardly—but not the ending of knowledge in the world where you have to function with knowledge. That which is holy, that which is sacred, which is truth, can only be when there is complete silence, when the brain itself has put thought in its right place. Out of that immense silence there is that which is sacred.

MEDITATION, if you understand what it is, is one of the most extraordinary things; but you cannot possibly understand it unless you have come to the end of seeking, groping, wanting something which you consider truth—which is your own projection. You cannot come to it unless you are no longer demanding experience at all, but are understanding the confusion in which one lives, the disorder of one's own life. In the observation of that disorder, order comes—which is not a blueprint. When you have done this—which in itself is meditation—then we can ask not only what meditation is, but also what meditation is not, because in the denial of that which is false, the truth is.

THE PHYSICAL ORGANISM has its own intelligence which is made dull through habits of pleasure. These habits destroy the sensitivity of the organism and this lack of sensitivity makes the mind dull. Such a mind may be alert in a narrow and limited direction and yet be insensitive. The depth of such a mind is measurable and is caught by images and illusions. Its very superficiality is its only brightness. A light and intelligent organism is necessary for meditation.

IN THE UNDERSTANDING of meditation there is love, and love is not the product of systems, of habits, of following a method. Love cannot be cultivated by thought. Love can perhaps come into being when there is complete silence, a silence in which the meditator is entirely absent; and the mind can be silent only when it understands its own movement as thought and feeling. To understand this movement of thought and feeling there can be no condemnation in observing it. To observe in such a way is discipline, and that kind of discipline is fluid, free, not the discipline of conformity.

WHAT IS MEDITATION? Before we go into that really quite complex and intricate problem we ought to be very clear as to what it is that we are after. We are always seeking something, especially those who are religiously minded. Even for the scientist, seeking has become quite an issue. This factor of seeking must be very clearly and definitely understood before we go into what meditation is and why one should meditate at all, what is its use and where does it get you.

The word "seek"—to run after, to search out—implies, does it not, that we already know, more or less, what we are after. When we say we are seeking truth, or we are seeking God if we are religiously minded, or we are seeking a perfect life and so on, we must already have in our minds an image or an idea. To find something after seeking it, we must already have known what its contour is, its color, its substance and so on. Isn't it implied in that word "seeking" that we have lost something and we are going to find it, and that when we find it we shall be able to recognize it; which means that we have already known it, that all we have to do is to go after it and search it out?

In meditation the first thing to realize is that it is no use to seek; for what is sought is predetermined by what you wish. If you are unhappy, lonely, in despair, you will search out hope, companionship, something to sustain you, and you will find it, inevitably.

IS THERE A MEDITATION which is not determined, practiced? There is, but that requires enormous attention. That attention is a flame and that attention is not something that you come to; it is attention *now* to everything, every word, every gesture, every thought; it is to pay complete attention, not partial. If you are listening partially now, you are not giving complete attention. When you are completely attentive there is no self, there is no limitation.

A RELIGIOUS LIFE is a life of meditation, in which the activities of the self are not.

CAN THE TOTALITY of the mind, the brain included, be completely still? People have asked this question, really very serious people, and they have not been able to solve it. They have tried tricks. They have said that the mind can be made still through the repetition of words. Have you ever tried repeating "Ave Maria" or those Sanskrit words, mantras, that some people bring over from India, repeating certain words to make the mind still? It does not matter what the word is, make it rhythmic, "Coca-Cola," any word—repeat it often and you will see that your mind becomes quiet; but it is a dull mind, it is not a sensitive mind, alert, vital, passionate. A dull mind, though it may say, "I have had a tremendous transcendental experience," is deceiving itself.

THE WHOLE POINT of meditation is not to follow the path laid down by thought to what it considers to be truth, enlightenment or reality. There is no path to truth. The following of any path leads to what thought has already formulated and, however pleasant or satisfying, it is not truth. It is a fallacy to think that a system of meditation, the constant practicing of that system in daily life for a few given moments, or the repetition of it during the day, will bring about clarity or understanding. Meditation lies beyond all this and, like love, cannot be cultivated by thought. As long as the thinker exists to meditate, meditation is merely a part of that self-isolation which is the common movement of one's everyday life.

THERE'S NO MEDITATOR in meditation. If there is, it is not meditation.

MEDITATION IS a state of mind which looks at everything with complete attention—totally, not just parts of it. And no one can teach you how to be attentive. If any system teaches you how to be attentive, then you are attentive to the system, and that is not attention.

WHEN YOU LOOK at a tree, or the face of your neighbor, or the face of your wife or husband, and if you look with that quality of mind that is completely quiet, then you will see something totally new. Such silence of the mind is not something that can be attained through any practice; if you practice a method you are still living within a very small space which thought has created, as the "me," the "I" practicing, advancing. That space is full of conflict, full of its own achievements and failures, and such a mind can never be quiet, do what it will.

MEDITATION IS EMPTYING the mind of the known. The known is the past. The emptying is not at the end of accumulation but rather it means not to accumulate at all. What has been is emptied only in the present, not by thought but by action, by the doing of "what is." The past is the movement of conclusion to conclusion, and the judgment of "what is" by the conclusion. All judgment is conclusion, whether it be of the past or of the present, and it is this conclusion that prevents the constant emptying of the mind of the known; for the known is always conclusion, determination.

The known is the action of will, and the will in operation is the continuation of the known, so the action of will cannot possibly empty the mind.

ALL OUR LIFE is based on thought which is measurable. It measures God, it measures its relationship with another through the image. It tries to improve itself according to what it thinks it should be. So unnecessarily we live in a world of measurement, and with that world we want to enter into a world in which there is no measurement at all. Meditation is the seeing of "what is" and going beyond it—seeing the measure and going beyond the measure.

MEDITATION IS THE EMPTYING of the content of consciousness. That is the meaning and the depth of meditation,
the emptying of all the content—thought coming to an end.

Meditation is the attention in which there is no registration.
Normally the brain is registering almost everything, the noise,
the words which are being used; it is registering like a tape.
Now is it possible for the brain not to register except that
which is absolutely necessary? Why should I register an insult?
Why? Why should I register flattery? It is unnecessary. Why
should I register any hurts? Therefore, register only that which
is necessary in order to operate in daily life—as a technician,
a writer and so on—but psychologically, do not register anything. In meditation there is no registration psychologically,
no registration except the practical facts of living, going to the
office, working in a factory, and so on—nothing else. Out of
that comes complete silence, because thought has come to an
end—except to function only where it is absolutely necessary.
Time has come to an end, and there is a totally different kind
of movement, in silence.

CAN YOU PRACTICE AWARENESS? If you are "practicing" awareness, then you are being inattentive. So, be aware of inattention, you do not have to practice. You do not have to go to Burma, China, India, places which are romantic but not factual. I remember once travelling in a car in India with a group of people. I was sitting in the front with the driver. There were three behind who were talking about awareness, wanting to discuss with me what awareness is. The car was going very fast. A goat was in the road, and the driver did not pay much attention and ran over the poor animal. The gentlemen behind were discussing what is awareness, but they never knew what had happened! You laugh, but that is what we are all doing.

IN THE TOTAL ATTENTION of meditation there is no knowing, no recognition, nor the remembrance of something that
has happened. Time and thought have entirely come to an
end, for they are the center which limits its own vision.

At the moment of light, thought withers away, and the
conscious effort to experience and the remembrance of it,
is the word that has been. And the word is never the actual.
At that moment—which is not of time—the ultimate is the
immediate, but that ultimate has no symbol, is of no person,
of no god.

THE WHOLE OF ASIA talks about meditation; it is one of their habits, as it is a habit to believe in God or something else. They sit for ten minutes a day in a quiet room and "meditate," concentrate, fix their mind on an image, an image created by themselves, or by somebody who has offered that image through propaganda. During those ten minutes they try to control the mind; the mind wants to go back and forth and they battle with it. They play that game everlastingly, and that is what they call meditation.

If one does not know anything about meditation, then one has to find out what it is—actually, not according to anybody, and that may lead one to nothing or it may lead one to everything. One must inquire, ask that question, without any expectation.

FOR MOST OF US, beauty is in something, in a building, in a cloud, in the shape of a tree, in a beautiful face. Is beauty "out there," or is it a quality of mind that has no self-centered activity? Because, like joy, the understanding of beauty is essential in meditation.

MEDITATION IS the emptying the mind of all thought, for thought and feeling dissipate energy; they are repetitive, producing mechanical activities which are a necessary part of existence. But they are only part, and thought and feeling cannot possibly enter into the immensity of life. Quite a different approach is necessary, not the path of habit, association and the known; there must be freedom from these. Meditation is the emptying of the mind of the known. It cannot be done by thought or by the hidden prompting of thought, nor by desire in the form of prayer, nor through the self-effacing hypnotism of words, images, hopes and vanities. All these have to come to an end, easily, without effort and choice, in the flame of awareness.

IT IS ONLY the still mind that understands that in a quiet mind there is a movement that is totally different, that is of a different dimension, of a different quality. That can never be put into words, because it is indescribable. What can be described is what comes up to this point, the point when you have laid the foundation and seen the necessity, the truth, and the beauty of a still mind.

MEDITATION IS the innocence of the present, and therefore it is always alone. The mind that is completely alone, untouched by thought, ceases to accumulate. So the emptying of the mind is always in the present. For the mind that is alone, the future—which is of the past—ceases. Meditation is a movement, not a conclusion, not an end to be achieved.

One must really understand this question of the past—the past as yesterday, through today, shaping tomorrow from what has been yesterday. Can that mind, which is the result of time, of evolution, be free of the past? Which is to die. It is only a mind that knows this, that can come upon this thing called meditation. Without understanding all this, to try to meditate is just childish imagination.

HAVE YOU EVER TRIED, during the day, to be watchful without correction, aware without choice, watching your thought, your motives, what you are saying, how you are sitting, the manner of your usage of words, your gestures— watching?

CAN THE MIND become quiet? I don't know what you are going to do about it when you see the problem, when you see the necessity, the truth of having this delicate, subtle mind, which is absolutely quiet. How is it to happen? This is the problem of meditation, because only such a mind is a religious mind. It is only such a mind that sees the whole of life as a unit, as a unitary movement, not fragmented. Therefore such a mind acts totally, not fragmentarily, because it acts out of complete stillness.

CAN THIS RADICAL inward revolution happen instantly? It can happen instantly when you see the danger of all this. It is like seeing the danger of a precipice, of a wild animal, of a snake; then there is instant action. But we do not see the danger of all this fragmentation which takes place when the "self," the "me," becomes important—and the fragmentation of the "me" and the "not me." The moment there is that fragmentation in yourself there must be conflict; and conflict is the very root of corruption. So, it behooves one to find out for oneself the beauty of meditation, for then the mind, being free and unconditioned, perceives what is true.

MEDITATION REALLY is a complete emptying of the mind. Then there is only the functioning of the body; there is only the activity of the organism and nothing else; then thought functions without identification as the "me" and the "not me." Thought is mechanical, as is the organism. What creates conflict is thought identifying itself with one of its parts which becomes the me, the self and the various divisions in that self. There is no need for the self at any time. There is nothing but the body, and freedom of the mind can happen only when thought is not breeding the "me."

ON THIS MORNING the quality of meditation was nothingness, the total emptiness of time and space. It is a fact and not an idea or the paradox of opposing speculations. One finds this strange emptiness when the root of all problems withers away. This root is thought, the thought that divides and holds. In meditation the mind actually becomes empty of the past, though it can use the past as thought. This goes on throughout the day and at night sleep is the emptiness of yesterday and therefore the mind touches that which is timeless.

MEDITATION IS EMPTYING the mind of the known. The known is the past. The emptying is not at the end of accumulation but rather it means not to accumulate at all. What has been is emptied only in the present, not by thought but by action, by the doing of "what is." The past is the movement of conclusion to conclusion, and the judgment of "what is" by the conclusion. All judgment is conclusion, whether it be of the past or of the present, and it is this conclusion that prevents the constant emptying of the mind of the known; for the known is always conclusion, determination.

MEDITATION IS one of the most serious things; you do it all day, in the office, with the family, when you say to somebody, "I love you," when you are considering your children. Then you educate them to become soldiers, to kill, to be nationalized, worshiping the flag, educating them to enter into this trap of the modern world; watching all that, realizing your part in it, all that is part of meditation. And when you meditate you will find in it an extraordinary beauty; you will act rightly at every moment; and if you do not act rightly at a given moment it does not matter, you will pick it up again— you will not waste time in regret. Meditation is part of life, not something different from life.

AS ONE TRAVELS over the world and observes the appalling conditions of poverty and the ugliness of man's relationship to man, it becomes obvious that there must be a total revolution. A different kind of culture must come into being. The old culture is almost dead and yet we are clinging to it. Those who are young revolt against it, but unfortunately have not found a way, or a means, of transforming the essential quality of the human being, which is the mind. Unless there is a deep psychological revolution, mere reformation on the periphery will have little effect. This psychological revolution—which I think is the only revolution—is possible through meditation.

To BE absolutely nothing is to be beyond measure.

BEAUTY MEANS SENSITIVITY—a body that is sensitive, which means the right diet, the right way of living, and you have all this, if you have gone that far. I hope you will, or are doing it now; then the mind will inevitably and naturally, unknowingly, become quiet. You can't make the mind quiet, because you are the mischief-maker, you are yourself disturbed, anxious, confused—how can you make the mind quiet? But when you understand what quietness is, when you understand what confusion is, what sorrow is and whether sorrow can ever end, and when you understand pleasure, then out of that comes an extraordinarily quiet mind; you don't have to seek it. You must begin at the beginning and the first step is the last step, and this is meditation.

WHAT IS THE significance of experience? Has it any significance? Can experience wake up a mind that is asleep, that has come to certain conclusions and is held and conditioned by beliefs? Can experience wake it up, shatter all that structure? Can such a mind—so conditioned, so burdened by its own innumerable problems and despairs and sorrows—respond to any challenge? Can it? And if it does respond, must not the response be inadequate and therefore lead to more conflict?

LOVE IS MEDITATION. Love is not a remembrance, an image sustained by thought as pleasure, nor the romantic image which sensuality builds; it is something that lies beyond all the senses and beyond the economic and social pressures of life. The immediate realization of this love, which has no root in yesterday, is meditation; for love is truth, and meditation is the discovery of the beauty of this truth.

WHEN THERE IS ONLY the organism without the self, perception, both visual and non-visual, can never be distorted. There is only seeing "what is" and that very perception goes beyond "what is." The emptying of the mind is not an activity of thought or an intellectual process. The continuous seeing of "what is" without any kind of distortion naturally empties the mind of all thought and yet that very mind can use thought when it is necessary. Thought is mechanical and meditation is not.

THE MIND AND THE BRAIN and the body in complete harmony must be silent—a silence that is not induced by taking a tranquilizer or by repeating words, whether it be "Ave Maria" or some Sanskrit word. By repetition your mind can become dull, and a mind which is in a stupor cannot possibly find what is true. Truth is something that is new all the time—the word "new" is not right, it is really "timeless."

There has to be silence. That silence is not the opposite of noise or the cessation of chattering; it is not the result of control, saying "I will be silent," which again is a contradiction. When you say "I will," there must be an entity who determines to be silent and therefore practices something which he calls silence; therefore there is a division, a contradiction, a distortion.

MEDITATION IS NOT the mere experiencing of something beyond everyday thought and feeling nor is it the pursuit of visions and delights. An immature and squalid little mind can and does have visions of expanding consciousness, and experiences which it recognizes according to its own conditioning. This immaturity may be greatly capable of making itself successful in this world and achieving fame and notoriety. The gurus whom it follows are of the same quality and state. Meditation does not belong to such as these. It is not for the seeker, for the seeker finds what he wants, and the comfort he derives from it is the morality of his own fears.

DO WHAT HE WILL, the man of belief and dogma cannot enter into the realm of meditation. To meditate, freedom is necessary. It is not meditation first and freedom afterwards; freedom—the total denial of social morality and values—is the first movement of meditation. It is not a public affair where many can join in and offer prayers. It stands alone, and is always beyond the borders of social conduct. For truth is not in the things of thought or in what thought has put together and calls truth. The complete negation of this whole structure of thought is the positive of meditation.

MEDITATION IS ALWAYS NEW. It has not the touch of the past for it has no continuity. The word "new" doesn't convey the quality of a freshness that has not been before. It is like the light of a candle which has been put out and relit. The new light is not the old, though the candle is the same. Meditation has a continuity only when thought colors it, shapes it and gives it a purpose. The purpose and meaning of meditation given by thought becomes a time-binding bondage. But the meditation that is not touched by thought has its own movement, which is not of time. Time implies the old and the new as a movement from the roots of yesterday to the flowing of tomorrow. But meditation is a different flowering altogether. It is not the outcome of the experience of yesterday, and therefore it has no roots at all in time. It has a continuity which is not that of time. The word "continuity" in meditation is misleading, for that which was, yesterday, is not taking place today.

THE MEDITATION of today is a new awakening, a new flowering of the beauty of goodness.

MEDITATION IS the ending of the word. Silence is not induced by a word, the word being thought. The action out of silence is entirely different from the action born of the word; meditation is the freeing of the mind from all symbols, images and remembrances.

THE EMPTY MIND cannot be purchased at the altar of de-
mand; it comes into being when thought is aware of its own
activities—not the thinker being aware of his thought.

SOURCES

page

3   The Only Revolution (New York: Harper & Row, 1970), p. 115.

4   Freedom from the Known (New York: Harper & Row, 1969), p. 116.

5   Krishnamurti's Notebook (New York: Harper & Row, 1976), p. 91.

6   The Impossible Question (London: Victor Gollancz, 1972), p. 72.

7   The Only Revolution, p. 41.

8   The Only Revolution, p. 45.

9   The Flight of the Eagle (New York: Harper & Row, 1972), p. 38.

10   Meditations 1969 (London: Krishnamurti Foundation Trust, 1969), p. 5.

12   The Flight of the Eagle, p. 46.

13   The Only Revolution, p. 37.

14   The Only Revolution, p. 15.

15   Krishnamurti's Notebook, p. 213.

16   The Awakening of Intelligence (London: Victor Gollancz, 1973), p. 475.

17   Meditations 1969, p. 10.

18   You Are the World. (New York: Harper & Row, 1972), p. 42.

19   The Only Revolution, p. 163.

20   The Awakening of Intelligence, p. 483.

21   Meditations 1969, p. 3.

22   Krishnamurti's Notebook, p. 225.

23   Beyond Violence (London: Victor Gollancz, 1973), p. 133.

24   Talks with American Students, p. 136.

25 The Only Revolution, p. 142.

26 The Only Revolution, p. 59.

27 The Awakening of Intelligence, p. 97.

28 Krishnamurti's Notebook, p. 126.

30 Meditations 1969, p. 8.

32 Krishnamurti's Notebook, p. 192.

33 The Only Revolution, p. 70.

34 The Only Revolution, p. 118.

35 Beginnings of Learning. (New York: Penguin Arkana, 1975), p. 240.

36 Meditations 1969, p. 11.

38 Krishnamurti's Notebook, p. 227.

39 The Awakening of Intelligence, p. 472.

40 Meditations 1969, p. 1.

41 Krishnamurti's Notebook, p. 177.

42 Krishnamurti's Notebook, p. 122.

43 The Only Revolution, p. 51.

44 The Awakening of Intelligence, p. 97.

45 Meditations 1969, p. 7.

46 Krishnamurti's Notebook, p. 91.

47 Talks in Europe 1967 (The Netherlands: Servire Wassenaar, 1969), p. 141.

48 Meditations 1969, p. 9.

50 Krishnamurti Foundation of America archives.

51 The Only Revolution, p. 33.

52 Talks with American Students (Boston: Shambhala Publications, Inc. 1970), p. 130.

53 Meditations 1969, p. 6.

54 Krishnamurti's Notebook, p. 171.

55   The Only Revolution, p. 155.

56   Krishnamurti's Notebook, p. 89.

57   The Only Revolution, p. 108.

58   Krishnamurti's Notebook, p. 160.

59   The Only Revolution, p. 146.

60   Krishnamurti's Notebook, p. 223.

61   Freedom from the Known, p. 116.

62   Krishnamurti's Notebook, p. 83.

63   The Only Revolution, p. 25.

64   The Impossible Question, p. 190.

65   Krishnamurti's Journal (London: Victor Gollancz, 1982), p. 58.

66   Krishnamurti Foundation of America Bulletin 32 (Ojai: Krishnamurti Foundation of America, 1977).

67   Beyond Violence, p. 54.

68   Krishnamurti in India 1970–71 (India: Krishnamurti Foundation India, 1971), p. 55.

69   The Flight of the Eagle, p. 39.

70   Talks and Dialogues in Sydney 1970 (Sydney: Krishnamurti Books, 1970), p. 76.

71   Krishnamurti in India 1970–71, p. 129.

72   The Only Revolution, p. 19.

74   The Awakening of Intelligence, p. 96.

75   The Wholeness of Life (San Francisco: Harper & Row, 1978), p. 142.

76   Beyond Violence, p. 156.

77   Meditations 1969, p. 6; last sentence: Krishnamurti's Journal, p. 72.

78   The Awakening of Intelligence, p. 96; Krishnamurti's Journal, p. 72.

79   Beyond Violence, p. 87.

80   Beyond Violence, p. 167.

81 The Awakening of Intelligence, p. 473.

82 Krishnamurti in India 1970–71, p. 129.

83 Beyond Violence, p. 167.

84 Freedom from the Known, p. 115.

85 The Beginnings of Learning, p. 250.

86 The Wholeness of Life, p. 145.

87 The Flight of the Eagle, p. 40.

88 Krishnamurti Foundation Trust Bulletin 4 (London: Krishnamurti Foundation Trust, 1969).

89 Freedom from the Known, p. 116.

90 Beyond Violence, p. 86.

91 Washington D. C. Talks 1985 (The Hague: Mirananda, 1988), p. 49.

92 Saanen 29th July 1973. Unpublished Talk: Krishnamurti Foundation Trust.

93 The Flight of the Eagle, p. 43.

94 Krishnamurti Foundation of America Bulletin 30 (Ojai: Krishnamurti Foundation of America).

95 Krishnamurti's Journal, p. 12.

96 Freedom from the Known, p. 116.

97 Bombay, February 11th, 1968. Unpublished talk, Krishnamurti Foundation Trust.

98 The Only Revolution, p. 93.

99 The Awakening of Intelligence, p. 482.

100 The Wholeness of Life, p. 144.

101 The Flight of the Eagle, p. 41.

102 The Only Revolution, p. 58.

103 Beyond Violence, p. 91.

104 The Awakening of Intelligence, p. 98.

105 Krishnamurti's Notebook, p. 163.

106 *The Awakening of Intelligence*, p. 78.

107 from "Meditation" to "achieved" *The Only Revolution*, p. 94.

107 from "One must" to "imagination" *Beyond Violence*, p. 117.

108 *You Are the World*, p. 153.

109 *The Awakening of Intelligence*, p. 97.

110 *Beyond Violence*, p. 166.

111 *Beginnings of Learning*, p. 250.

112 *The Awakening of Intelligence*, p. 6.

113 *The Only Revolution*, p. 93.

114 *The Flight of the Eagle*, p. 46.

115 *The Awakening of Intelligence*, p. 2.

116 *Krishnamurti's Journal*, p. 73.

117 *The Awakening of Intelligence*, p. 98.

118 *The Flight of the Eagle*, p. 38.

119 Krishnamurti Foundation of America archives.

120 *Beginnings of Learning*, p. 250.

121 *Beyond Violence*, p. 130.

122 *The Only Revolution*, p. 86.

123 *The Only Revolution*, p. 86.

124 *The Only Revolution*, p. 128.

125 *The Only Revolution*, p. 129.

126 *The Only Revolution*, p. 121.

127 *The Only Revolution*, p. 94.

Books by J. Krishnamurti

Can Humanity Change?: J. Krishnamurti in Dialogue with Buddhists
Many have considered Buddhism to be the religion closest in spirit to J. Krishnamurti's spiritual teaching—even though the great teacher was famous for urging students to seek truth outside organized religion. This record of a historic encounter between Krishnamurti and a group of Buddhist scholars provides a unique opportunity to see what the great teacher had to say himself about Buddhist teachings.

Facing a World in Crisis: What Life Teaches Us in Challenging Times
Facing a World in Crisis presents a selection of talks that Krishnamurti gave on how to live and respond to troubling and uncertain times. His message of personal responsibility and the importance of connecting with the broader world is presented in a nonsectarian and nonpolitical way. Direct and ultimately life-affirming, this book will resonate with readers looking for a new way to understand and find hope in challenging times.

Freedom, Love, and Action
In *Freedom, Love, and Action*, Krishnamurti points to a state of total awareness beyond mental processes. With his characteristic engaging, candid approach, Krishnamurti discusses such topics as the importance of setting the mind free from its own conditioning; the possibility of finding enlightenment in everyday activities; the inseparability of freedom, love, and action; and why it is best to love without attachment.

Inward Revolution: Bringing about Radical Change in the World
Here, J. Krishnamurti inquires with the reader into how remembering and dwelling on past events, both pleasurable and painful, give us a false sense of continuity, causing us to suffer. His instruction is to be attentive and clear in our perceptions and to meet the challenges of life directly in each new moment.

Meditations
This classic collection of brief excerpts from Krishnamurti's books and talks presents the essence of his teaching on meditation—a state of attention, beyond thought, that brings total freedom from authority and ambition, fears and separateness.

Talks with American Students
In 1968—a time when young Americans were intensely questioning the values of their society—Krishnamurti gave a series of talks to college students in the United States and Puerto Rico, exploring the true meaning of freedom and rebellion. Collected in this book, these lectures are perhaps even more compelling today, when both adults and young people are searching for the key to genuine change in our world.

This Light in Oneself: True Meditation
These selections present the core of Krishnamurti's teaching on meditation, taken from discussions with small groups, as well as from public talks to large audiences. His main theme is the essential need to look inward, to know ourselves, in order really to understand our own—and the world's—conflicts. He offers timeless insights into the source of true freedom and wisdom.